CW01668934

aritime &
oastguard
gency

Code of Practice for Controlling Risks due to Hand-transmitted Vibration on Ships

LONDON: TSO

a Williams Lea company

Published by TSO (The Stationery Office), part of Williams Lea,
and available from:

Online
www.tsoshop.co.uk

Mail, Telephone, Fax & E-mail
TSO
PO Box 29, Norwich, NR3 1GN
Telephone orders/General enquiries: 0333 202 5070
Fax orders: 0333 202 5080
E-mail: customer.services@tso.co.uk
Textphone 0333 202 5077

TSO@Blackwell and other Accredited Agents

Published for the Maritime and Coastguard Agency under licence from the Controller of Her Majesty's Stationery Office

The Maritime and Coastguard Agency wishes to acknowledge the expert contribution made by the Institute of Sound and Vibration Research, based at Southampton University in producing this code

ISBN 978 0 11 553090 6

First published 2009
Eleventh impression 2022

Printed in the United Kingdom for TSO
J003885977

Preface

The EC Physical Agents (Vibration) Directive (2002/44/EC) is implemented for land based workers in Great Britain by the Control of Vibration at Work Regulations 2005 (SI 2005/1093) and for land based workers in Northern Ireland by the Control of Vibration at Work (Northern Ireland) Regulations 2005 (SR(NI) 2005 No.397)

For workers on ships Directive 2002/44/EC is implemented by the Merchant Shipping and Fishing Vessels (Control of Vibration at Work) Regulations 2007 (SI 2007/3077).

This Code of Practice is intended to assist those concerned with designing, building and owning or managing ships to comply with the Merchant Shipping and Fishing Vessels (Control of Vibration at Work) Regulations 2007. This Code is based upon existing guidance to the EU Directives (European Commission, 2008) and the Control of Vibration at Work Regulations 2005 (Health and Safety Executive, 2005a), but with the information edited and packaged in the context of the provisions of the Merchant Shipping and Fishing Vessels (Control of Vibration at Work) Regulations 2007 (herein referred to as the "2007 Vibration Regulations")
as they apply to hand-transmitted vibration.

Contents

1 Introduction

The Merchant Shipping and Fishing Vessel (Control of Vibration at Work) Regulations 2007 (the "2007 Vibration Regulations") implement a 2002 European Union Directive on the minimum health and safety requirements regarding the exposure of workers to the risks arising from occupational vibration. To implement the EU Directive for land-based workers, UK regulations have already been introduced by the Health and Safety Executive, but these land-based regulations do not apply to the master and crew of a UK ship in respect of normal shipboard activities.

The 2007 Vibration Regulations extend the provisions of Directive 2002/44/EC to workers, irrespective of nationality, who are employed on UK registered vessels irrespective of whether they are operating on inland waters or at sea and also irrespective of where in the world they are operating. The Vibration Regulations include provisions for:

- action values and limit values for exposure to vibration,
- risk assessment,
- elimination of or, where this is not reasonably practicable, reduction of exposure to vibration,
- actions to be taken at action values and limit values,
- prohibition on exceeding limit values,
- information, instruction and training for vibration-exposed workers,
- health surveillance, and
- consultation with workers.

Those primarily affected by the vibration regulations will be operators and managers of ships, fishing vessels, and other marine craft, including yachts, work boats etc. registered in the UK on which paid workers are employed.

The 2007 Vibration Regulations will apply also to charities and similar organisations that operate vessels, but only when there are paid workers on such vessels.

The main provisions of the vibration regulations may be seen in the overview of Appendix A. Employers are required to identify which of their employees may be at risk from vibration, to assess the degree of risk and to introduce measures to eliminate or minimise that risk. The provisions of the regulations will be enforced by means of inspections carried out by surveyors or inspectors from the Maritime and Coastguard Agency. As the regulations are intended to improve the health and safety of workers on board UK ships and fishing vessels, the regulations contain sanctions for non-compliance.

This Code of Practice is intended to help those concerned with designing, building, operating or managing vessels to understand their responsibilities under the Merchant Shipping and Fishing Vessels (Control of Vibration at Work) Regulations 2007 as they apply to hand-transmitted vibration, also known as hand-arm vibration.

2 Scope of the Code

This Code of Practice deals with:

- the assessment of risk from hand-transmitted vibration onboard ships,
- the measurement and evaluation of hand-transmitted vibration,
- the assessment of the severity of exposures to hand-transmitted vibration,
- the identification of controls to eliminate or reduce exposures to hand-transmitted vibration,
- the involvement of crew members in the control hand-transmitted vibration risks, including the provision of information and training, and
- the provision of health monitoring and surveillance for hand-transmitted vibration.

The provisions of this Code are not intended to apply to passenger spaces, but if crew are required to work in such spaces they will be regarded as crew work areas.

3 Purpose of the Code

The objectives of this code of practice are to:

- explain the duties of employers regarding the assessment and control of health risks associated with exposure to hand-transmitted vibration in the maritime environment;
- provide sufficient information to enable employers to assess the risks of injury to seafarers from hand-transmitted vibration;
- set out measures to be taken to control that risk, either by appropriate design and use of equipment or by the use of methods to limit exposures to hand-transmitted vibration;
- set out the requirements to monitor the health of seafarers;
- discuss the employer's duties to inform seafarers of the risks and consequences of exposure to hand-transmitted vibration, and to provide adequate training for the safe use of vessels, machinery and tools.

It is assumed that the readers of this code will include ship owners and managers, masters, officers, and other interested parties such as ship designers and builders. A degree of technical knowledge is assumed, but it is recognised that any single individual is unlikely to have the necessary knowledge and skills to deal effectively with all of the objectives of this code. To fulfil all the requirements of the vibration regulations, an employer may need to use the services of a technical specialist, who may be found either in-house or contracted-in.

4 Application of the Code

The 2007 Vibration Regulations apply to all vessels registered in the United Kingdom on which workers are employed, whether in UK inland waters or the territorial sea or anywhere else in the world. The guidance in this Code applies to all such vessels.

This Code is also relevant to United Kingdom vessels involved in civil protection services or public service activities, and to non-UK-registered ships and vessels when they are in UK waters.

Privately-owned pleasure craft fall within the scope of this Code if there are paid crew on such craft.

The Code covers the safety of crew, regardless of nationality. It applies to crew when they are on-board for the purpose of work, whether the vessel is in port, or at sea, including time when they are off duty.

5 Effects of hand-transmitted vibration on crew

Hand-transmitted vibration (also known as hand-arm vibration) is caused by vibration transmitted into the hands and arms through the palms and fingers. This may arise from the use of hand-held or hand-guided power tools and machines, or from controls used to operate vessels or vessel machinery. Workers whose hands are regularly exposed to hand-transmitted vibration may suffer from damage to the tissues of the hands and arms, which cause the symptoms collectively known as hand-arm vibration syndrome (HAVS) (Griffin, 1990; Griffin and Bovenzi, 2004).

In advice to employers on the 2005 Vibration Regulations (Health and Safety Executive, 2005a), the HSE summarise the state of knowledge and say:

The symptoms include:

- tingling and numbness in the fingers;
- not being able to feel things properly;
- loss of strength in the hands;
- fingers going white (blanching) and becoming red and painful on recovery – particularly in the cold and wet, and probably only in the tips at first.

For some people, symptoms may appear after only a few months of exposure, but for others they may take a few years. The symptoms are likely to get worse with continued exposure to vibration and may become permanent.

The effects on exposed people can include:

- pain, distress and sleep disturbance;
- inability to do fine work (e.g., assembling small components) or everyday tasks (e.g., fastening buttons);
- reduced ability to work in cold or damp conditions (i.e., most outdoor work) that could trigger attacks of finger blanching;
- reduced grip strength, which might affect the ability to work safely.

These effects can severely limit the jobs an affected person is able to do, as well as family and social activities."

Further information on the signs and symptoms of the HAVS can be found in Appendix G. The vascular and neurological components of the HAVS are prescribed diseases in the UK under the Industrial Injuries Disability Benefit Scheme.

The risks from hand-transmitted vibration are increased if equipment produces higher magnitudes of vibration and if there is prolonged and regular use of vibratory equipment.

It has been shown that vibration hazards can be controlled and the risks reduced by good management. The costs of such controls need not be high and can be offset by the benefits of keeping workers healthy. Additionally, the vibration control measures may lead to improved efficiency.

5.1 Exposure action values and exposure limit values

The 2007 Vibration Regulations establish minimum standards for controlling the risks to seafarers from hand-transmitted vibration. The vibration regulations set:

i. an exposure action value for daily vibration exposure of 2.5 m/s^2 *A*(8),above which employers are required to implement measures to control the hand-arm vibration risks of their workforce;

ii. a daily exposure limit value of 5 m/s^2 *A*(8) above which workers must not be exposed.

The exposure action value and exposure limit value are each standardised to an eight hour reference period.

The risk of injury from hand-transmitted vibration is reduced where exposures are below the exposure action value, but there may still be risk of injury at lower exposure levels.

The regulations place specific responsibilities on employers to ensure that risks from hand-transmitted vibration are eliminated or reduced to a minimum. These responsibilities are summarised in Appendix A, and are discussed in the following sections.

6 Assessment of risks

6.1 Survey method

The Merchant Shipping and Fishing Vessels (Health and Safety at Work) Regulations 1997 (SI 1997/2962) require a suitable and sufficient risk assessment to be made of the risks of the health and safety of workers arising in the normal course of their activities or duties, for the purpose of identifying:

i. groups of workers at particular risk in the performance of their duties;

ii. the measures to be taken to comply with the employer's duties under the Regulations.

As part of this risk assessment, to comply with the 2007 Vibration Regulations the employer should:

i. identify workers who may be at risk from hand-transmitted vibration;

ii. decide if workers are likely to be exposed above the daily exposure action value or the daily exposure limit value;

iii. identify the available methods for controlling the identified risks;

iv. identify the steps that will be taken to control and monitor the risks;

v. record the assessment, the steps that have been taken, and their effectiveness.

6.2 Identification of workers at risk

A good starting point would be to perform a survey of the activities that are carried out by the vessel's crew so as to:

- determine which, if any, work activities involve regular exposure to hand-transmitted vibration;

- list all the tools and equipment available to the crew that may produce hand-transmitted vibration, locate the equipment handbooks and find out whether there are any warnings of vibration risks;
- find out which workers use the tools and equipment that may produce hand-transmitted vibration, and determine the jobs that each tool is used for;
- ask workers which tools or equipment produces high levels of vibration or uncomfortable strains on the hands or arms.

Appendix B provides information on the vibration magnitudes that can be expected on some tools that are known to present risks from hand-transmitted vibration.

The HSE recommend that employers "group activities according to whether they are high, medium or low risk. Plan your action to control risks for the employees at greatest risk first. Your rough groupings could be based on the following:

High risk (above the exposure limit value)
Employees who regularly operate:

- hammer action tools for more than about one hour per day;
- some rotary and other action tools for more than about four hours per day.

Employees in this group are likely to be above the exposure limit value set out in the Regulations. The limit value could be exceeded in a much shorter time in some cases, especially where the tools are not the most suitable for the job.

Medium risk (above the exposure action value)
Employees who regularly operate:

- hammer action tools for more than about 15 minutes per day;
- some rotary and other action tools for more than about one hour per day.

Employees in this group are likely to be exposed above the exposure action value set out in the Regulations."

It will certainly be necessary to take action if individual employees are operating impact or percussive tools for more than about 15 minutes per day, or rotary action tools for more than one hour per day, unless the employer has evidence to show that the exposure is not high enough to exceed the exposure action value. Hammer-action tools with the highest emissions can exceed the exposure action value in less than five minutes. Rotary action tools with the highest emissions can exceed the exposure action value within about fifteen minutes (Health and Safety Executive, 2005c).

The HSE (Health and Safety Executive, 2005a) advise that "The rough groupings described above should be enough for you to do a basic risk assessment which will enable you to decide whether exposures are likely to exceed the exposure action value and exposure limit value and to allow you to plan and prioritise your control actions effectively.

Alternatively, you may choose either to use available vibration data or to have measurements made to estimate exposures if you want to be more certain of whether the risk is high, medium or low. A more detailed exposure assessment may help you:

- decide which control actions might be most effective and practicable in reducing vibration exposure;
- be more certain whether exposures are likely to exceed the action or limit values;
- check whether your controls are effective.

Section 6.3 outlines the necessary steps to performing a detailed exposure assessment.

It is important to keep workers and their representatives involved and informed in the assessment of vibration risks. An effective partnership with workers will help to ensure the information used for the risk assessment is based on realistic assessments of the work being carried out and the time taken to do that work.

6.3 Measurement and evaluation of exposures to hand-transmitted vibration

It is not always necessary to measure a workers' exposure to vibration if the basic risk assessment described in the previous section has been carried out.

When employers need to check whether exposures are likely to exceed the action or limit values, it may be possible to estimate vibration magnitudes from manufacturer's data or from other published data sources (see Section 6.3.3.3). If it is not possible to obtain adequate information from other sources on the vibration produced by a tool or work process it may be necessary to make measurements of vibration at the workplace. It may be necessary to make measurements where:

- a vibrating machine is used for an unusual purpose, of which the manufacturer has limited experience and so cannot provide information;
- it is not clear from the limited information available whether the exposure action value or exposure limit value is likely to be exceeded;
- an employer needs to check the effectiveness of actions taken to control hand-transmitted vibration exposures.

The quantity that is evaluated for comparison with the exposure action value and the exposure limit value is the daily vibration exposure, $A(8)$. This is expressed in units of metres per second squared (m/s^2 r.m.s.) and represents the 8-hour energy equivalent vibration magnitude for a worker, including all hand-transmitted vibration exposures during the day.

The factors that govern a person's daily vibration exposure are the frequency-weighted magnitude of the vibration and the length of time the person is exposed to it. The greater the magnitude or the longer the duration of exposure, the greater will be the person's vibration exposure

6.3.1 Competent persons

The risk assessment and the evaluation and assessment of vibration exposures should be performed by a 'competent person'. This person may be an employee of the ship owner/operator, or an external consultant contracted to the ship owner/operator.

The assessor should have a thorough understanding of the vibration regulations. He or she should also have adequate general knowledge of vessel structure and layout, and be acquainted with the work schedules and practices used onboard the vessel being surveyed.

If sufficient data are available from tool manufacturers or other sources it should be possible for an otherwise technically competent non-specialist to make an adequate estimate of vibration magnitudes, using the information and sources cited in this section.

Vibration measurement is a complex task. Whether the measurements are performed in-house, or by a specialist consultant, whoever makes the vibration measurements should have sufficient competence and experience. Persons performing measurements must have a thorough understanding of the measurement and analysis of hand-transmitted vibration according to BS EN ISO 5349-1:2001, as well as training and practical experience in performing vibration testing on hand-tools.

Specialist consultants or engineers who are employed to assess vibration exposures should be able to demonstrate that:

- they have practical experience in the assessment of hand-transmitted vibration;
- their equipment complies with the requirements of BS EN ISO 8041:2005 and is in current calibration: measuring instrument and calibrators should be returned to the manufacturer or other competent organisation capable of providing a calibration check traceable to a national standard laboratory at intervals not exceeding two years.

It is recommended that such consultants or engineers have a quality system in place that covers these activities and is compliant with the current version of BS EN ISO 9001.

6.3.2 Determining duration of exposure

Before the daily vibration exposure, *A*(8), can be estimated, it is necessary to know the total daily duration of exposure to the vibration from each tool or process being used. You should be careful to count only the time that the worker is exposed to vibration. A period when a worker has put the equipment down or is holding it but not operating it so as to be exposed to hand-transmitted vibration should not be counted.

The contact time or trigger time is the time that the hands are actually exposed to the vibration from the tool or workpiece. The trigger time is often much shorter than the overall "time on the job" and is often over-estimated by operators. The method used for estimating trigger times depends on whether the tool usage is continuous or intermittent:

Continuous operation of a tool or machine:
Tasks carried out on ships can involve the continuous operation of a tool or machine over a long period. Examples include the operation of an outboard motor with the steering or throttle handle, or surface preparation for repainting using a chipping hammer, hand grinder, or needle gun. In these cases the work should be observed to determine the length of time the tool or machine is operating during a representative working day. A stopwatch or video recording can be useful.

Intermittent tool operation:
If a task involves intermittent repeated operations, such as drilling a large number of holes, it should be possible to count the number of operations that occur during a working day (e.g., the number of holes drilled). The average duration should be estimated by observing the trigger time over several operations, then multiplied by the number of holes drilled so as to estimate the total trigger time.

6.3.2.1 Work Patterns

Work patterns need careful consideration. For example, some workers may only use vibratory tools for specific periods in a day or week. Typical usage patterns should be established, as these will be required to calculate a person's likely vibration exposure.

6.3.3 Determining exposure magnitude

6.3.3.1 Definition of vibration magnitude

The vibration magnitude is expressed in terms of the frequency-weighted acceleration of the surface of the handle or workpiece that is in contact with the hand, as defined in BS EN ISO 5349-1:2001.

The vibration is defined by the amplitude and frequency of the oscillations arising from external and internal forces. The vibration amplitude is usually expressed in acceleration units (metres per second per second, or m/s^2) because most vibration transducers produce an output that is related to acceleration. The vibration frequency is expressed in cycles per second, which is more usually known as hertz (abbreviated to Hz).

For hand-transmitted vibration, the frequencies thought to be important range from about 8 Hz to 1000 Hz. However, because the risk of damage to the hand is not equal at all frequencies, a frequency-weighting is used to represent the likelihood of damage from the different frequencies. For hand-transmitted vibration, the same frequency-weighting curve is used for all three axes (see Figure 1). The frequency-weighting incorporates band limiting filters to attenuate accelerations below 8 Hz and above 1000 Hz.

To get a complete picture of the vibration on a surface, vibration must be measured in three axes, as illustrated in Figure 2. The acceleration magnitude (a_{hwj}) for axis j (where j = x, y or z) is the root-mean-square average of the frequency-weighted acceleration time history, calculated according to:

$$a_{hwj} = \left(\frac{1}{T} \int_0^T a_{hwj}^2(t) dt \right)^{\frac{1}{2}}$$

where $a_{hwj}(t)$ is the frequency-weighted acceleration in axis j as a function of time t, and T is the duration of the measurement.

The value used for the assessment of exposure is the vibration total value, a_{hv}, which combines the frequency-weighted acceleration magnitudes in the axes x, y and z, using:

$$a_{hv} = \sqrt{a_{hwx}^2 + a_{hwy}^2 + a_{hwz}^2}$$

6.3.3.2 Making measurements

Human exposure to hand-transmitted vibration should be evaluated using the method defined in BS EN ISO 5349-1:2001. Practical guidance on using the method for the measurement of vibration at the workplace is given in BS EN ISO 5349-2:2001.

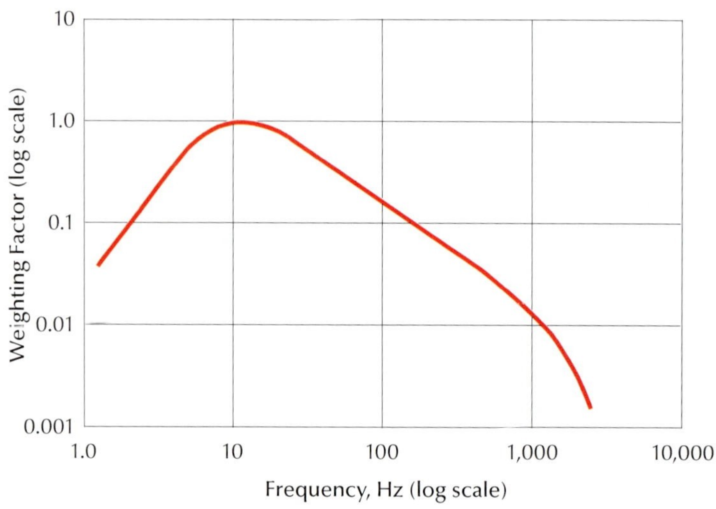

Figure 1 The Wh frequency weighting for hand-transmitted vibration

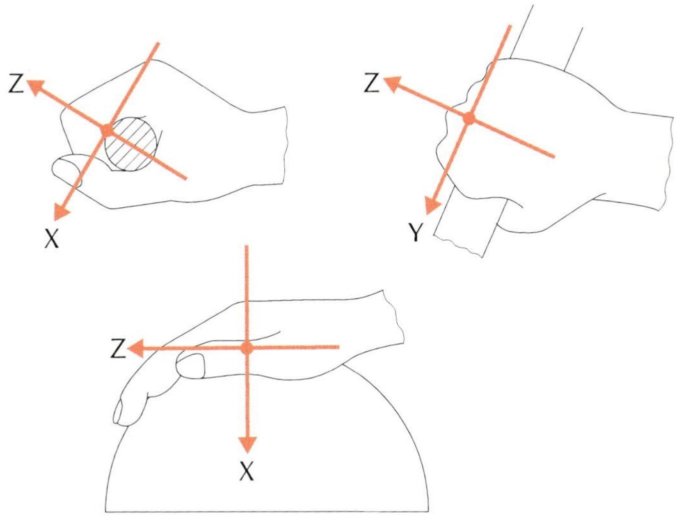

Figure 2 Axes for measuring hand-transmitted vibration, modified from BS EN ISO 5349:2001

Measurements should be obtained so as to produce vibration values that are representative of the average vibration for a tool or process throughout the operator's working period. The operating conditions and measurement periods should be selected to achieve this.

Where tools are held in both hands, measurements must be made at both hand positions and the highest value used for determining vibration exposure.

6.3.3.2.1 Measuring Instrumentation

The measurement of vibration on a tool handle, workpiece or control requires suitable accelerometers (vibration transducers), and an instrument that provides signal conditioning and analysis and/or recording of acceleration time histories for later analysis. Hand-transmitted vibration measuring equipment should comply with BS EN ISO 8041:2005 (Human response to vibration – measuring instrumentation).

All equipment should be in current calibration, traceable to national standards, and wherever possible calibration checks, by mounting the transducers on portable or laboratory calibrators, should be performed before and after measurements.

The instrumentation can comprise a self-contained meter or a sub-system that connects to a personal computer with suitable analysis software. It is desirable to use an instrument that records and displays acceleration time histories, since this makes it possible for the operator to directly observe problems due to overloading, mounting or connecting to the transducers.

It is important that accelerometers are carefully selected. Vibration must be measured in three axes using either a tri-axial accelerometer, or three single-axis accelerometers orientated in orthogonal directions. The vibration on hand-held and hand-guided machines can be very high and can easily overload unsuitable transducers. Fixing transducers to the machine handles or workpiece requires mounting systems that are rigid, lightweight, and compact. Further information and guidance on transducer selection and mounting methods can be found in BS EN ISO 5349-2:2001.

6.3.3.3 Use of manufacturer's emission data

Amongst other requirements, the European "Machinery Directive" (European Commission, 2006) requires manufacturers, importers, and suppliers of tools and machines to provide information on vibration emissions at the hand. This vibration emission should be stated in the information or instructions that accompany the tool or machine.

General principles for the evaluation of vibration emission of hand-held tools are given in BS EN ISO 20643:2008. Harmonised vibration test codes based on this standard have been produced by European and International standards bodies, such as the EN ISO 28662 and EN ISO 28927 series for pneumatic and other non-electric tools and the EN 60745 series for electric tools. Declared emission values allow purchasers to compare machines tested to the same standardised test code. The emission values can show when there are large differences between machines, so that high-vibration tools can be avoided. Emission data from manufacturers can also indicate how much vibration is likely to enter a person's hands when using a particular power tool. This may be useful to help make an estimate of daily exposure and an assessment of risk.

Most current vibration test codes report the vibration total value, a_{hv}, summed over three axes as required by the vibration regulations. However, it is important to be aware that some older vibration test codes only report the vibration magnitude measured in the dominant vibration axis, and these will underestimate the vibration total value (see PD CEN/TR 15350:2006 for more information).

6.3.3.4 *Use of other data sources*

There are other sources of information on vibration magnitudes that may allow an employer to decide whether the exposure action value or the exposure limit value is likely to be exceeded.

Relevant trade associations may have useful vibration data, and there are international vibration databases on the Internet that may provide the information needed for an initial vibration risk assessment.

Other sources of vibration data include specialist vibration consultants and government bodies. Some data can also be found in various technical or scientific publications and some data on typical real-use vibration may be available on manufacturer's web sites. There are several websites in English that hold manufacturers' standard vibration emission data and/or values measured in "real use" for a range of machines, including hand-held tools commonly used on ships, for example:

- http://www.operc.com/havtec/havinfo.asp
- http://www.vibration.db.umu.se/HavSok.aspx?lang=en

Employers should use vibration information for the equipment (make and model) they use. However, if this is not available they may use values relating to similar equipment as a starting point, replacing the data with more accurate values when they become available.

When choosing published vibration information the following factors should be taken into account:

- the type of equipment (e.g. hand-held grinder);
- the class of equipment (e.g. power or size);
- the power source (e.g. pneumatic, hydraulic, electric or combustion engine);
- any anti-vibration features (e.g. suspended handles);
- the task the equipment was used for when producing the vibration information;
- the speed at which it was operated;
- the type of material on which it was used.

When using published vibration data it is good practice to try to compare data from two or more sources.

6.3.4 Calculating daily exposures

6.3.4.1 *Daily vibration exposure*

The daily vibration exposure, $A(8)$, depends on the frequency-weighted magnitude and the square root of the exposure duration:

$$A(8) = a_{hv}\sqrt{\frac{T}{T_0}}$$

where a_{hv} is the vibration magnitude (in m/s^2), T is the daily duration of exposure to the vibration magnitude a_{hv} and T_0 is the reference duration of eight hours

Examples of the calculation of daily vibration exposures are given in Appendix C.

6.3.4.2 *Partial vibration exposures*

If a person is exposed to more than one source of vibration (perhaps because they use two or more different tools or processes during the day) then the partial vibration exposures are calculated from the magnitude and duration for each one. The partial vibration values are combined to give the overall daily exposure value, $A(8)$, for that person. An example of the calculation of daily vibration exposures is given in Appendix C.

Each partial vibration exposure represents the contribution of a particular source of vibration (tool or process) to the worker's total daily exposure. Knowledge of the partial exposure values will help priorities to be established: the tools or processes with the highest partial vibration exposure values are those that should be given priority for control measures.

6.3.4.3 *Uncertainty of daily exposure evaluations*

There are many factors that introduce uncertainty into the evaluation of hand-transmitted vibration exposure. Uncertainties in vibration exposure evaluations are dependent on many factors (see BS EN ISO 5349-2:2001) including:

- instrument calibration uncertainty;
- mounting of accelerometers, and accelerometer mass;
- location of accelerometers;
- accuracy of source data (e.g. manufacturer's emission data);

- variation within and between machine operators (e.g. experience, operating technique or physique);
- ability of the worker to reproduce typical work during measurements;
- repeatability of the work task;
- variations in the machine (e.g. is there a need for maintenance, has the machine been warmed-up?);
- wear of inserted components or abrasives (e.g. is the saw-blade sharp, is the abrasive disc worn?).

The uncertainty associated with instrumentation and calibration, and mounting of accelerometers will usually be small compared to the uncertainties due to selection of measurement location and variability in the work operation. When making vibration measurements, the assessor should determine the main sources of uncertainty and the resulting variation in vibration magnitudes. Multiple measurements should be made of each operation, and the standard deviation of the measured magnitudes should be calculated for the dominant sources of uncertainty (e.g. different operators; variation on inserted components such as grinding wheels or the material itself that is being worked on). The reported vibration magnitude should be the arithmetic mean of the measurements, but the standard deviation should also be recorded so as to indicate the extent of the uncertainty (BS EN ISO 5349-2:2001).

If the exposure duration is estimated (e.g., based on information from the worker) or the vibration magnitude is estimated (e.g. based on information from the tool manufacturer), the uncertainty in the evaluation of daily exposure can be great. Employers should take the possible sources of uncertainty into account in their risk assessments. A larger uncertainty increases the risk since workers may be exposed to higher than expected magnitudes of vibration.

6.4 Survey reporting

The vibration regulations require employers to keep a record of the risk assessment and control actions. They also require employers to keep health records for workers under health surveillance and to review and update the health surveillance regularly.

Comprehensive records should also be made of any vibration measurements that have been carried out. The information that should be reported is specified in BS EN ISO 5349-2:2002. Appendix F provides a suggested format for reporting hand-transmitted vibration measurements according to the 2007 Vibration Regulations. Such a report might usefully be carried onboard the vessel to which it applies.

Records of risk assessments, control actions, health records and measurement reports must be retained by the employer. Although the 2007 Vibration Regulations do not specify how long they should be kept it would be prudent to retain records for 40 years, or until all current employees have retired from work.

7 Avoiding or reducing exposure to hand-transmitted vibration

The European Framework Directive 89/391/EEC on the introduction of measures to encourage improvements in the safety and health of workers at work (European Commission, 1990) suggests that the following hierarchy should be adopted for establishing priorities in a programme of preventative measures:

i. avoid risks;

ii. evaluate risks that cannot be avoided;

iii. reduce the risks at source;

iv. adapt the work to the individual (especially with respect to the design of work places, the choice of work equipment and the choice of working and production methods) so as to reduce effects on health.

v. adapt to technical progress;

vi. replace the dangerous by the non-dangerous or the less dangerous;

vii. develop a coherent overall prevention policy that covers technology, organization of work, working conditions, social relationships and the influence of factors related to the working environment;

viii. give collective protective measures priority over individual protective measures;

ix. give appropriate instructions to the workers.

7.1 Developing a control strategy

The risk assessment undertaken by an employer should enable methods for controlling exposure to be identified. While assessing the vibration exposures, it is important to think about the work processes that cause them. Understanding why workers are exposed to high magnitudes of hand-transmitted vibration will help to identify methods for reducing or eliminating the risks.

The important stages in this management process are:

- identifying the chief sources of vibration;
- ranking them in terms of their contribution to the risk;
- identifying and evaluating potential solutions in terms of practicability and cost;
- establishing targets which can be realistically achieved;
- allocating priorities and establishing an 'action programme';
- defining management responsibilities and allocating adequate resources;
- implementing the programme;
- monitoring progress;
- evaluating the programme.

The approach that is taken to reduce risks from hand-transmitted vibration will depend on the practical aspects of the particular processes being carried out and on the current levels of exposure.

The controls may need to be adapted for workers who are at particular risk of injury (e.g., those workers who are more susceptible to vibration injury and show signs of developing injury at exposures below the exposure action value).

Ranking the contributions of different exposures

Example: use of partial vibration exposure to rank risks

A worker uses two tools, a grinder with an in-use vibration emission of 7 m/s^2 r.m.s. and a chipping hammer with an in-use emission of 16 m/s^2 r.m.s. The grinder is used for a total of 2½ hours per day and the chipping hammer for 15 minutes:

Grinder (*7 m/s^2 for 2½ hours*):	$A_1(8) = 3.9$ m/s^2
Chipping hammer (*16 m/s^2 for 15 minutes*):	$A_2(8) = 2.8$ m/s^2
Total exposure:	$A(8) = 4.8$ m/s^2

Although the chipping hammer has a greater vibration magnitude than the grinder, the partial exposure values show that the use of the grinder accounts for the greater proportion of the worker's overall vibration exposure. Therefore, initially, the grinder should be the main focus for risk reduction.

7.2 Involvement of workers

The successful management of risks relies on the support and involvement of workers, and in particular their representatives. Representatives can provide a channel of communication with the workforce and assist workers in understanding and using health and safety information.

While some hand-transmitted vibration control solutions will be straightforward, others will require changes to the way in which work is organised. Such changes can only be dealt with in consultation with workplace representatives.

Effective consultation relies on:

- the sharing of information about health and safety measures with workers;
- workers being given the opportunity to express their views and contribute in a timely fashion to the resolution of health and safety issues;
- the views of workers being valued and taken into account.

Consultation can result in better control solutions being identified and solutions that are better understood by the workers. You will be relying on workers to make the control measures effective. Subject to adequate training and supervision, workers have a duty to make correct use of machinery and to cooperate with the employer to enable them to ensure that their environment and the working conditions are safe, such that risks to safety and health are minimised and where possible eliminated. The process of consultation encourages worker involvement and their co-operation with control measures and so ensures that controls are more likely to be implemented successfully.

7.3 Risk controls

There are various engineering, management, and other methods to be considered when looking for control solutions.

7.3.1 Clothing

7.3.1.1 Protection from cold

Low body temperatures reduce blood circulation and increase the risk of finger blanching. Outdoor working in cold weather should be avoided if possible.

The temperature in an indoor workplace should provide reasonable comfort without the need for special clothing and should normally be at least 16°C. You should avoid machines that might make the hands cold (e.g. steel-bodied machines or pneumatic tools that blow exhaust air over the operator's hands).

Warm clothing and gloves should be provided if there is an increased risk due to cold. Gloves and other clothing should be assessed for good fit and for effectiveness in keeping the hands and body warm and dry in the working environment.

7.3.1.2 Anti-vibration gloves

Some commercially available gloves are marketed as 'anti-vibration', indicating that they have been tested and found to meet the requirements of BS EN ISO 10819:1997. For most powered hand-tools the reduction in frequency-weighted vibration magnitude provided by anti-vibration gloves is negligible, and they can increase the vibration at some frequencies. Gloves should therefore not be relied on to provide protection from hand-transmitted vibration. Gloves can, however, be useful to protect the hands of vibration-exposed workers from cold, by helping to maintain the blood circulation (see below).

7.3.2 Substitution of other working methods

It may be possible to find alternative work methods that eliminate or reduce exposure to vibration. This may involve mechanisation or automation of tasks, or substitution of alternative work processes. To keep up-to-date on the methods available, regular checks should be made with relevant trade associations, other industry contacts, equipment suppliers and trade journals.

7.3.3 Equipment selection/purchasing/maintenance

7.3.3.1 Equipment selection

You should make sure that equipment selected or allocated for tasks is suitable and can do the work efficiently. Equipment can be unsuitable because it has insufficient capacity and is likely to take much longer to complete the task and expose workers to vibration for longer than is necessary.

Selection of consumables (e.g. abrasives for grinders and sanders) or tool accessories (such as drill bits, chisels and saw blades) can affect vibration exposure. Some manufacturers supply accessories designed to reduce vibration exposure. To keep up-to-date on the tools, consumables and accessories available it is advisable to check regularly with equipment suppliers, relevant trade associations, other industry contacts, and trade journals.

7.3.3.2 Purchasing policy

Employers should make sure that their purchasing department has a policy on purchasing suitable equipment that takes into account both vibration emission and operating requirements.

Power tool manufacturers (and importers, suppliers, and tool hire firms) should be able to help in the selection of the most suitable and safest tools for particular tasks. They should provide useful information and advice about tool vibration, selection, and management. They have duties to reduce risks from vibration to a minimum and to help employers with information on managing vibration risks that they have been unable to eliminate by design.

Anyone supplying power tools for use in Europe must comply with the Machinery Directive (European Commission, 2006), which requires them to provide information on:

- the vibration emission (as reported in the instruction handbook);
- how the emission value has been obtained.

The supplier may also be able to offer technical support where required, including advice on:

- any applications of the equipment that are believed to increase the risk of injury from hand-transmitted vibration;
- how to use the equipment safely and any training requirements for safe use;
- any training (to operators, maintenance staff etc.) recommended to control hand-transmitted vibration exposures;
- how to use the equipment for specific tasks;
- the need for any personal protective equipment when operating the machinery;
- how to maintain the tool in good condition;
- any vibration reduction features.

When selecting tools, employers should also consider ergonomic factors and other hazards such as:

- tool weight, handle design and comfort;
- grip forces, ease of use and handling;
- cold from grip surfaces or from exhaust air on pneumatic tools;
- noise and dust.

Manufacturers or suppliers may be willing to loan sample tools on trial. Make use of this opportunity and take account of workers' opinions based on practical trials. The efficiency of the tool is important: a tool that takes a long time to do the job will not be popular, and could result in a higher vibration exposure than an efficient tool with a greater vibration magnitude. However, tools that are too powerful for the job could result in exposure to unnecessarily high vibration magnitudes.

7.3.3.3 Maintenance

Regular servicing of power tools and other work equipment will often help keep vibration magnitudes down to the minimum necessary, so it is important to:

- keep cutting tools sharp;
- dress grinding wheels correctly by following the manufacturer's recommendations;
- lubricate moving parts in accordance with manufacturer's recommendations;
- replace worn parts;
- carry out any necessary balance checks and corrections;
- replace anti-vibration mounts and suspended handles before they deteriorate (look for deterioration or the cracking, swelling and softening or hardening of rubber mounts);
- check and replace defective vibration dampers, bearings and gears.

7.3.4 Workstation design

7.3.4.1 Jigs and anti-vibration handles

Jigs and similar aids incorporating anti-vibration mounts can help avoid the need to hold vibrating surfaces.

'Anti-vibration' handles may reduce the vibration, but incorrect selection of this type of handle may actually increase the vibration at the hand, so only use handles that are endorsed by the tool manufacturer.

7.3.4.2 Resilient materials

Wrapping rubber or other resilient materials around vibrating handles is not recommended. Resilient materials may amplify vibration at some frequencies and increase vibration exposure. No modification should be made to a tool or machine without the manufacturer's agreement since it might compromise safety.

7.3.4.3 Grip and push forces

Reductions in gripping or pushing forces exerted through the hand tend to reduce the vibration passing into the user's hands and arms. However, grip and push forces may be required to support the tool or workpiece, to control or guide the machine, or to achieve high work-rates. The actual forces applied can be greater than is necessary for efficient work because of incorrect equipment selection, inadequate maintenance, insufficient training or port work station design.

Some methods of reducing grip and push forces are:

- where heavy workpieces are ground by hand at pedestal grinders, support for the whole piece will mean that the worker needs only to guide into the wheel, rather than support all the weight.
- tension chains (sometimes called balancers) and manipulators can be used to support vibrating tools such as heavy drills, grinders, nut runners, nailing guns (in some cases) and pneumatic chisels, thus relieving the operator from supporting the tools weight;
- changes in the texture and material of a grip surface may allow the operator to use a smaller grip force to control the tool.

7.3.5 Work schedules

To control the risks from hand-transmitted vibration, employers may need to limit the time workers are exposed to vibration from some tools or processes. It is recommended that work is planned to avoid workers being exposed to vibration for long, continuous periods.

Employers should make sure that new work patterns are adequately supervised, to ensure that workers do not drift back to the older work patterns.

7.3.6 Training and Information to workers

Employers should provide operators and supervisors with information on:

- the potential injury arising from the work equipment in use;
- the exposure limit values and the exposure action values;
- the results of the vibration risk assessment and any vibration measurements;
- the control measures being used to eliminate or reduce risks from hand-transmitted vibration;
- safe working practices to minimise exposure to mechanical vibration;
- why and how to detect and report signs of injury;
- why and how to report machines in need of maintenance;
- how and when to scrap inserted tools or consumables that contribute to excessive vibration exposures;
- the circumstances in which workers are entitled to health surveillance.

Employers rely on the operators of vibrating tools and processes to make their control measures effective. Consultations should be held with the workers and their representatives when implementing control measures. Workers have a duty to cooperate when employers take action to comply with European health and safety directives.

Workers should be trained in the best working techniques, for example to help avoid excessive gripping, pushing, and guiding forces and to ensure the tools are operated safely and with optimum efficiency. They also need to be trained to recognise when a machine is in need of maintenance.

With some tools, the operator's hands must be in the correct position to avoid increased vibration exposure. Many vibration-reduced tools, such as breakers with suspended handles, produce high vibration emissions if the operator pushes down too hard while operating the tool.

The manufacturer should be able to give advice on any training requirements, and may offer training for operators. Workers can also be encouraged to rest the tool as much as possible on the material being worked (or in the case of hand-held workpieces, on any support provided) and to hold it with a light but safe grip.

Training and supervision will be required to ensure that workers are protecting themselves against the development of vibration-related disease. They should be encouraged to report any symptoms that may be associated with vibration or the use of power tools, etc. If they are taking part in a health surveillance scheme then this may provide a regular opportunity for one-to-one discussion of the vibration hazard and how to reduce the risk of injury.

Workers should also be advised on the impact of non-work activities on the risks to their health. They should be encouraged to stop or cut-down on smoking, which can impair blood circulation. Workers should also be aware that the use of power tools for do-it-yourself work in the home or activities such as motorbike riding will add to daily vibration exposures and so increase the risk of developing an injury from hand-transmitted vibration.

7.4 Monitoring and reassessment

7.4.1 How to find out if the hand-transmitted vibration controls are working

Employers will need to review their hand-transmitted vibration controls periodically to ensure they are still relevant and effective. They should:

- check regularly that managers and workers are still carrying out the programme of controls that have been introduced;
- talk frequently to managers, supervisors, workers and safety or worker representatives about whether there are any vibration problems with the equipment or the way it is being used;
- check the results of health surveillance and discuss with the occupational health provider whether the controls appear to be effective or need to be changed.

7.4.2 When should the risk assessment be repeated?

The risks from hand-transmitted vibration, and how you control them, will need to be reassessed whenever there are changes in the workplace that may affect the level of exposure, such as:

- the introduction of different machinery or processes;
- changes in the work pattern or working methods;
- changes in the number of hours worked with the vibrating equipment;
- the introduction of new vibration control measures.

The risks should also be reassessed if there is evidence (e.g., from health surveillance) that the existing controls are not effective. The extent of the reassessment will depend on the nature of the changes and the number of people affected by them. A change in the duration of exposure or work patterns may require a recalculation of the daily exposure for the people affected, but will not necessarily alter the vibration magnitudes. The introduction of new machinery or processes may require a full reassessment.

It is good practice to review risk assessments and work practices at regular intervals, even if nothing obvious has changed. There may be new technology, tool designs or ways of working that would allow further reductions of risk.

8 Health Surveillance

Health surveillance involves putting in place systematic, regular, and appropriate procedures for the detection of work-related ill health, and acting on the results. The aims are primarily to safeguard the health of workers (including identifying and protecting individuals at increased risk), but also to check the long-term effectiveness of control measures.

8.1 When is health surveillance required?

Employers should provide appropriate health surveillance where the risk assessment indicates a risk to worker health. The vibration regulations require health surveillance to be instituted for workers who are at risk from vibration injury where:

- the exposure of workers to vibration is such that a link can be established between that exposure and an identifiable illness or harmful effects on health;
- it is probable that the illness or the effects occur in a worker's particular working conditions;
- there are tested techniques for the detection of the illness or the harmful effects on health.

In any event, all workers whose daily vibration exposure exceeds the daily exposure action value are entitled to appropriate health surveillance.

8.2 How is health surveillance managed?

Basic health surveillance consists of a simple health monitoring system for collecting information about early symptoms of ill health using a questionnaire.

MCA Marine Guidance Note 353 (M+F) suggests that "it may help to keep costs down if employers carry out this function themselves by using a questionnaire, referring any positive responses to an occupational health provider".

Alternatively, an employer could ask an occupational health service provider to provide a complete service on their behalf. Examples of questionnaires that can be used by employers or by health professionals are available from the following websites:

- http://www.hse.gov.uk/vibration/hav/advicetoemployers/healthsurveillance.htm
- http://www.vibrisks.soton.ac.uk/ (see Epidemiological Tools)

Further information on health surveillance is provided in Appendix H.

8.3 What to do if injury or disease is identified?

Where, as a result of health surveillance, a worker is found to have an identifiable disease or adverse health effect that is considered by a doctor or occupational health-care professional to be the result of exposure to mechanical vibration at work, then certain duties fall upon the employer.

8.3.1 Information for the worker

The worker must be informed, by the doctor or other suitably qualified person, of the results of his or her own personal health surveillance. The worker may request that these health records be made available to some other person of his or her own choice. Workers shall be given information and advice regarding any health surveillance that they should undergo following the end of exposure.

8.3.2 Employer actions

Where health surveillance is carried out by a third party, the employer will need to be informed of any significant findings from the health surveillance as they relate to a seafarer's fitness for work involving exposure to vibration. Reports on an individual employee should contain only information on fitness to continue with work, unless that individual worker consents to the release of his or her medical information. The employers should also expect to be informed of any significant health surveillance findings in an anonymous form (e.g. for groups of employees).

Any adverse findings place duties upon the employer.

- The employer shall review the hand-transmitted vibration risk assessment;
- The employer shall review the measures provided to eliminate or reduce risks from hand-transmitted vibration exposure;
- The employer shall take into account the advice of the occupational healthcare professional or other suitably qualified person or the competent authority in implementing any measures required to eliminate or reduce risks from hand-transmitted vibration exposure, including the possibility of assigning the worker to alternative work where there is no risk of further exposure;
- Health surveillance should be continued with special attention to the health status of other seafarers with similar exposure. On a case by case basis, the competent doctor or occupational health care professional or the Maritime and Coastguard Agency may propose that exposed persons undergo a medical examination.

9 Responsibility (persons on whom duties are imposed)

9.1 Employers' duties

The vibration regulations place duties on employers to ensure that risks to workers from hand-transmitted vibration are eliminated or reduced to a minimum. There may be several different employers responsible for the crew of a ship, and not all of them will have control of the operation of the ship or the activities of the crew.

When an employer does not have direct control of activities that impose a risk due to hand-transmitted vibration the responsibility for ensuring that the duties outlined in this Code of Practice are carried out is extended to any other persons that do have control or responsibility for such activities.

9.2 Workers' duties

As well as the responsibilities placed on the employer, the vibration regulations place a responsibility on every worker to make full and proper use of all protective clothing and equipment provided by the employer, and to follow all the instructions and training that the employer has provided.

9.3 Prohibition of levy on any worker

Regulation 21 of the vibration regulations makes it clear that the costs of anything done or provided in pursuance of any specific requirement of the regulations cannot be passed on to any worker.

10 Definitions

Certain definitions from the 2007 Vibration Regulations are given immediately below.

Civil protection services

Include the fire and rescue services, ambulance services, and search-and-rescue services provided by any other person or organisation.

Employer

A person or corporate body by whom a worker is employed on a ship under a contract of employment.

Public service activities

Include the activities of HM Coastguard, HM Revenue and Customs, the armed forces, immigration officers, police, prison officers, and the security and intelligence services.

Worker

Any person employed on a ship under a contract of employment, including a trainee or apprentice other than any person who is training in a commercial yacht or sail training vessel. Throughout this Code of Practice, the words employee, seafarer and crew member are also used to mean worker.

The remainder of the definitions deal with hand-transmitted vibration and are arranged alphabetically.

Daily vibration exposure, A(8)

The 8-hour energy equivalent vibration total value for a worker in meters per second squared (m/s^2), including all hand-transmitted vibration exposures during the day.

Declared vibration emission

The vibration value provided by machine manufacturers to indicate the vibration likely to occur on their machines. The declared vibration emission value should be obtained using a standardised test code, and has to be included in the machine's instructions.

Exposure action value

A value for a workers daily exposure to hand-transmitted vibration, *A*(8) of 2.5 m/s^2 r.m.s., above which the risks from vibration exposure must be controlled.

Exposure limit value

A value for a workers daily exposure to hand-transmitted vibration, *A*(8) of 5.0 m/s^2 r.m.s., above which workers should not be exposed.

Exposure duration

The duration per day that a worker is exposed to a vibration source.

Frequency weighting

A filter applied to vibration measurements to reflect the frequency-dependence of the risk of damage to the body. The W_h weighting (defined in EN ISO 5349-1:2001) is used for hand-transmitted vibration.

Hand-arm vibration

The mechanical vibration that, when transmitted to the human hand-arm system, entails risks to the health and safety of workers, in particular vascular, bone or joint, neurological or muscular disorders.

Hand-transmitted vibration

Mechanical vibration (or shock) applied or transmitted directly to the hand-arm system, usually through the hand or fingers.

Health surveillance

Putting in place systematic, regular and appropriate procedures for the detection of work-related ill health, and acting on the results.

Partial vibration exposure

The contribution of an operation to the daily vibration exposure in m/s^2. The partial vibration exposure relates to the daily exposure from an individual tool or process. Where a worker is only exposed to vibration from one tool or process then the daily vibration exposure is equal to the partial vibration exposure.

11 Bibliography

11.1 U.K. Statutory Instruments

Statutory Instrument No. 1995/3163. The Reporting of Injuries, Diseases and Dangerous Occurrences Regulations 1995. The Stationary Office, ISBN 0110537513.

Statutory Instrument No. 1997/2962. The Merchant Shipping and Fishing Vessels (Health and Safety at Work) Regulations 1997. The Stationary Office, ISBN 0110653459.

Statutory Instrument No. 2005/1093. The Control of Vibration at Work Regulations 2005. The Stationary Office, ISBN 0110727673.

Statutory Instrument No. 2007/3077. The Merchant Shipping and Fishing Vessels (Control of Vibration at Work) Regulations 2007. The Stationary Office, ISBN 0110789091.

11.2 Guidance publications

European Commission (2008) Non-binding guide to good practice with a view to implementation of Directive 2002/44/EC on the minimum health and safety requirements regarding the exposure of workers to the risks arising from physical agents (vibrations). European Commission, ISBN 978 9279075339.

Health and Safety Executive (1998) Hard to handle: Hand-arm vibration – managing the risk video. HSE Books, ISBN 0717618811

Health and Safety Executive (1999) Health surveillance at work (HSG61, 2nd edition). HSE Books. ISBN 071761705X

Health and Safety Executive (2005a) Control the risks from hand-arm vibration: Advice for employers on the Control of Vibration at Work Regulations 2005. (Leaflet INDG175, rev2), HSE Books, ISBN 07176 61172

Health and Safety Executive (2005b) Hand-arm vibration: Advice for workers (Pocket card INDG296, rev1). HSE Books, ISBN 0717661180

Health and Safety Executive (2005c) Hand-arm Vibration – The Control of Vibration at Work Regulations 2005. Guidance on Regulations (L140). HSE Books, ISBN 0717661253

Health and Safety Executive (2008) Providing health surveillance. http://www.hse.gov.uk/vibration/hav/advicetoemployers/healthsurveillance.htm

Maritime and Coastguard Agency (2007a) The Merchant Shipping and Fishing Vessels (Control of Vibration at Work) Regulations 2007. Marine Guidance Note MGN 353. MCA, Southampton.

Maritime and Coastguard Agency (as amended) Code of Safe Working Practices for Merchant Seamen. The Stationary Office.

11.3 Standards and technical guides

(Note: British Standards are subject to periodic updating; use the most recent version.)

BS EN ISO 5349-1:2001. Mechanical vibration – Measurement and evaluation of human exposure to hand-transmitted vibration – Part 1: General requirements. British Standards Institution.

BS EN ISO 5349-2:2001. European Committee for Standardization (2001) Mechanical vibration – Measurement and evaluation of human exposure to hand-transmitted vibration – Part 2: Practical guidance for measurement at the workplace. British Standards Institution.

BS EN ISO 8041:2005. Human response to vibration – measuring instrumentation. British Standards Institution.

BS EN ISO 10819:1996. Mechanical vibration and shock – Hand-arm vibration – Method for the measurement and evaluation of the vibration transmissibility of gloves at the palm of the hand. British Standards Institution.

BS EN 12096:1997. Mechanical vibration – Declaration and verification of vibration emission values. British Standards Institution.

BS ISO 14835-1:2005 Mechanical vibration and shock — Cold provocation tests for the assessment of peripheral vascular function — Part 1: Measurement and evaluation of finger skin temperature. British Standards Institution.

BS ISO 14835-2:2005 Mechanical vibration and shock — Cold provocation tests for the assessment of peripheral vascular function — Part 2: Measurement and evaluation of finger systolic blood pressure. British Standards Institution.

BS EN ISO 20643:2008. Mechanical vibration – Hand-held and hand-guided machinery – Principles for evaluation of vibration emission. British Standards Institution.

CEN/CR 1030-1:1995. Hand-arm vibration – Guidelines for vibration hazards reduction – Part 1: Engineering methods by design of machinery. European Committee for Standardisation.

CEN/CR 1030-2:1995. Hand-arm vibration – Guidelines for vibration hazards reduction – Part 2: Management measures at the workplace. European Committee for Standardisation.

EN ISO/TS 15694:2004 Mechanical vibration and shock — Measurement and evaluation of single shocks transmitted from hand-held and hand-guided machines to the hand-arm system. European Committee for Standardisation.

PD CEN/TR 15350:2006. Mechanical vibration — Guideline for the assessment of exposure to hand-transmitted vibration using available information including that provided by manufacturers of machinery. British Standards Institution.

ISO 13091-1:2001 Mechanical vibration – Vibrotactile perception thresholds for the assessment of nerve dysfunction – Part 1: Methods of measurement at the fingertips. International Organization for Standardization.

ISO 13091-2:2003 Mechanical vibration – Vibrotactile perception thresholds for the assessment of nerve dysfunction – Part 2: Analysis and interpretation of measurements at the fingertips. International Organization for Standardization.

11.4 EU Directives

European Commission (1989) Council Directive 89/656/EEC of 30 November 1989 on the minimum health and safety requirements for the use by workers of personal protective equipment at the workplace (third individual directive within the meaning of Article 16 (1) of Directive 89/391/EEC).

European Commission (1990) On the minimum health and safety requirements for the manual handling of loads where there is a risk particularly of back injury to workers (fourth individual Directive within the meaning of Article 16(1) of Directive 89/391/EEC). Council Directive 90/269/EEC of 29 May 1990.

European Commission (2002) Directive 2002/44/EC of the European parliament and of the Council of 25 June 2002 on the minimum health and safety requirements regarding the exposure of workers to the risks arising from physical agents (vibration) (sixteenth individual Directive within the meaning of Article 16(1) of Directive 89/391/EEC)

European Commission (2006) Directive 2006/42/EC of the European Parliament and of the Council of 17 may 2006 on Machinery, and amending Directive 95/16/ec (recast).

11.5 Web sites

http://www.humanvibration.com. General information on human-vibration including links to various human-vibration websites

http://www.hse.gov.uk/vibration/hav/index.htm. Detailed information on risks due to hand-arm vibration in industry.

11.6 Scientific publications

Bovenzi,M. (2008) Vibration-induced white finger and cold response of digital arterial vessels in occupational groups with various patterns of exposure to hand-transmitted vibration. Scandinavian Journal of Work, Environment & Health, 24:138-144.

Bovenzi,M. (2002) Finger systolic blood pressure indices for the diagnosis of vibration-induced white finger. International Archives of Occupational and Environmental Health, 75:20-28.

Griffin,M.J. (2004) Minimum health and safety requirements for workers exposed to hand-transmitted vibration and whole-body vibration in the European Union; a review. Occupational and Environmental Medicine; 61, 387-397.

Griffin,M.J. (1990, 1996) Handbook of human vibration. Published: Academic Press, London, ISBN: 0-12-303040-4.

Griffin,M.J. (1997) Measurement, evaluation, and assessment of occupational exposures to hand-transmitted vibration. Occupational and Environmental Medicine, 54, (2), 73-89.

Griffin,M.J. (1998) Evaluating the effectiveness of gloves in reducing the hazards of hand-transmitted vibration. Occupational and Environmental Medicine, 55, (5), 340-348.

Griffin,M.J., Bovenzi,M. (2002) The diagnosis of disorders caused by hand-transmitted vibration: Southampton Workshop 2000. International Archives of Occupational and Environmental Health, 75, (1-2), 1-5.

Lindsell,C.J., Griffin. M.J. (1998) Standardised diagnostic methods for assessing components of the hand-arm vibration syndrome. HSE research report CRR 197/1998.

Mason,H., Poole,K. (2004) Clinical testing and management of individuals exposed to hand-transmitted vibration: an evidence review. Faculty of Occupational Medicine of the Royal College of Physicians, ISBN 1 86016 203 7.

Mansfield,N.J. (2004) Human Response to Vibration ISBN 0-4152-8239-X

Palmer,K.T., Griffin,M.J., Bednall,H., Pannett,B., Coggon,D. (2000) Prevalence and pattern of occupational exposure to hand transmitted vibration in Great Britain: findings from a national survey. Occupational and Environmental Medicine, 57, (4), 218-228.

Palmer,K.T., Griffin,M.J., Bendall,H., Pannett,B., Cooper,C., Coggon,D. (2000) The prevalence of sensorineural symptoms attributable to hand-transmitted vibration in Great Britain: a national postal survey. American Journal of Industrial Medicine, 38, 99-107.

Palmer,K.T., Griffin,M.J., Syddall,H., Pannett,B., Cooper,C., Coggon,D. (2000) Prevalence of Raynaud's phenomenon in Great Britain and its relation to hand transmitted vibration: a national postal survey. Occupational and Environmental Medicine, 57, (7), 448-452.

Palmer,K.T., Griffin,M.J., Syddall,H., Pannett,B., Cooper,C., Coggon,D. (2001) Risk of hand-arm vibration syndrome according to occupation and source of exposure to hand-transmitted

Palmer,K.T., Haward,B., Griffin,M.J., Bednall,H., Coggon,D. (2000) Validity of self reported occupational exposure to hand transmitted and whole body vibration. Occupational and Environmental Medicine, 57, (4), 237-241.

Stayner, R.M. (2003) Isolation and auto-balancing techniques for portable machines. HSE research report RR 078/2003.

Appendix A

Summary of responsibilities defined by the Merchant Shipping and Fishing Vessels (Control of Vibration at Work) Regulations 2007

Regulation no.	Person responsible	When	Requirement
Regulation 6	Employer	Potential risk from hand-arm vibration	**Determination and assessment of risk:** Use someone who is competent to assess the hand-arm vibration risk. Be in possession of the risk assessment. Identify measures required for control of exposure and worker information and training. Keep the risk assessment up to date.
Regulation 7	Employer	Risks from vibration	**Avoiding or reducing exposure:** Take general actions to eliminate exposures or reduce them to a minimum.
		Exposures above the **exposure action value**	Establish and implement programme of measures to eliminate, or reduce to a minimum, exposures to hand-arm vibration risks.
		Exposures above the **exposure limit value**	Take immediate action to prevent exposure above the limit value. Identify why the exposure limit value has been exceeded.
		Workers at particular risk	Adapt to requirements of workers at particular risk.

Regulation no.	Person responsible	When	Requirement
Regulation 8	Employer	Workers at risk from hand-arm vibration	**Worker information and training:** For all workers exposed to hand-arm vibration risks.
Regulation 10	Employer	Workers at risk from hand-arm vibration	**Worker consultation and participation:** To consult, in a balanced way and in good time, workers and their representatives on risk assessment, control measures health surveillance and training.
Regulation 9	Doctor or suitably qualified person	Where ill health is identified	**Health Surveillance:** Inform worker of results of health surveillance. Provide information and advice to worker regarding any health surveillance which he should undergo following the end of exposure. Provide significant findings of health surveillance to employer.
	Employer	Where ill health is identified	Review risk assessment. Further eliminate or reduce risks. Review the health status of similarly exposed workers.
	Employer	Exposures above the exposure action value	Workers are entitled to appropriate health surveillance.

Appendix B

Information on emission values for common tools

Figure B.1 shows sample data based on workplace vibration measurements of total vibration values, a_{hv} on some hand tools that might be found in the marine sector. These data, reported in European Commission (2008), are for illustration only and may not be representative of machine use in all circumstances.

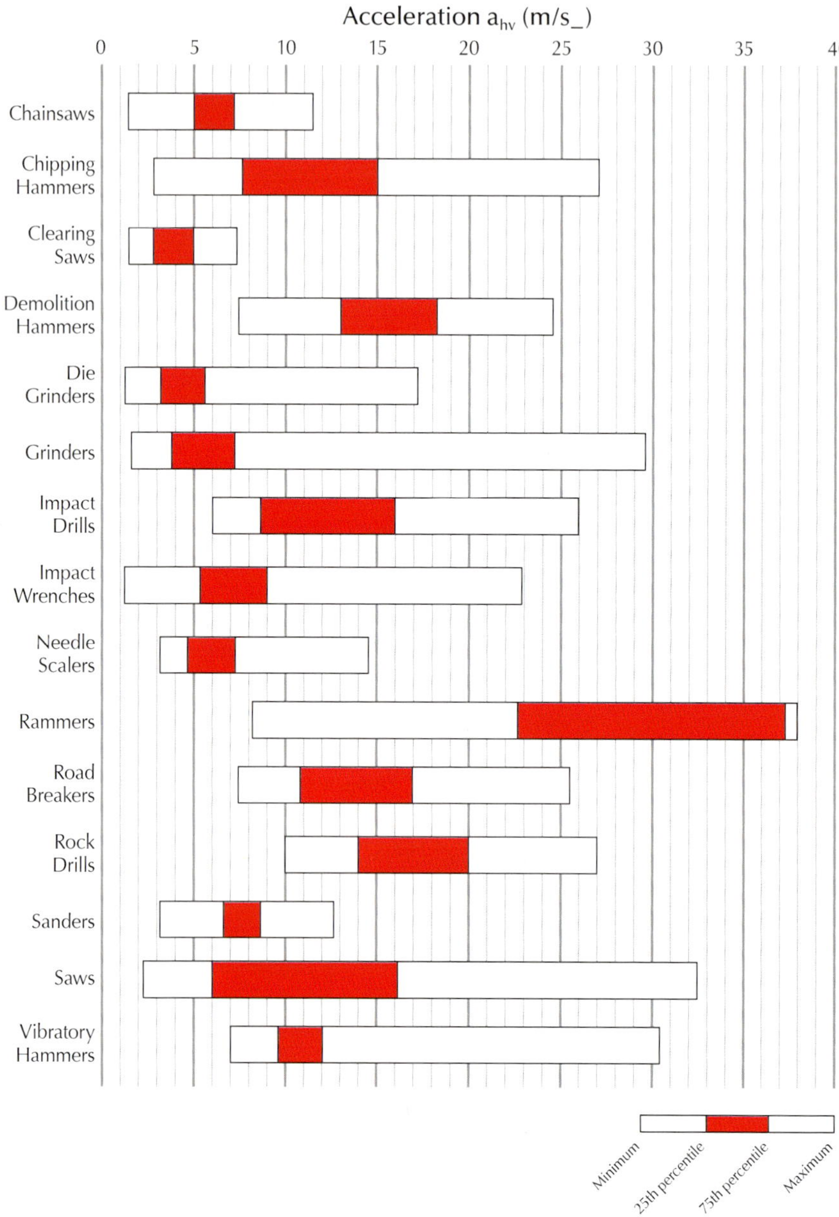

Figure B.1 Sample workplace vibration measurements on typical vibratory powered hand tools, reproduced from European Commission (2008). The 25th and 75th percentile points show the vibration magnitude that 25% or 75% of samples are equal to or below.

Appendix C

Worked Examples

Some worked examples are provided below. Further information and examples on the calculation of daily hand-transmitted vibration exposures can be found in PD CEN/TR 15350:2006.

C.1 Where just one machine is used

The daily vibration exposure, $A(8)$, for a worker carrying out one process or operating one tool can be calculated from a magnitude and exposure time, using the equation:

$$A(8) = a_{hv}\sqrt{\frac{T}{T_0}}$$

where a_{hv} is the vibration magnitude (in m/s² r.m.s.), T is the daily duration of exposure to the vibration magnitude a_{hv} and T_0 is the reference duration of eight hours. Like vibration magnitude, the daily vibration exposure has units of metres per second squared (m/s² r.m.s.).

Example 1

Use of a needle scaler for a total of 2½ hours a day. The vibration on a specific needle scaler when in use is 6.5 m/s² r.m.s. The daily exposure $A(8)$ is given by:

$$A(8) = 6.5\sqrt{\frac{2.5}{8}} = 3.6 \text{ m/s}^2 \text{ r.m.s}$$

This daily exposure of 3.6 m/s² r.m.s. is above the exposure action value but below the exposure limit value.

C.2 Where more than one machine is used

If a crew member is exposed to more than one source of vibration then partial vibration exposures are calculated from the magnitude and duration for each source.

The overall daily vibration exposure can be calculated from the partial vibration exposure values, using:

$$A(8) = \sqrt{A_1(8)^2 + A_2(8)^2 + A_3(8)^2 + \ldots}$$

where $A_1(8)$, $A_2(8)$, $A_3(8)$, etc. are the partial vibration exposure values for the different vibration sources.

Example 2

Use of three tools during a working day:

i. An angle grinder: 4 m/s^2 for 2½ hours

ii. An angle cutter for 3 m/s^2 for 1 hour

iii. chipping hammer 20 m/s^2 for 15 minutes

The partial vibration exposures for the three tasks are:

i. Angle grinder: $A_{grinder}(8) = 4\sqrt{\frac{2.5}{8}} = 2.2 \text{ m/s}^2$

ii. Angle cutter: $A_{cutter}(8) = 3\sqrt{\frac{1}{8}} = 1.1 \text{ m/s}^2$

iii. Chipping hammer: $A_{chipper}(8) = 20\sqrt{\frac{15}{8 \times 60}} = 3.5 \text{ m/s}^2$

The daily vibration exposure is then given by:

$$A(8) = \sqrt{A_{grinder}(8)^2 + A_{cutter}(8)^2 + A_{chipper}(8)^2}$$

$$= \sqrt{2.2^2 + 1.1^2 + 3.5^2}$$

$$= \sqrt{4.8 + 1.2 + 12.3}$$

$$= \sqrt{18.3} \quad = 4.3 \text{ m/s}^2$$

A daily exposure of 4.3 m/s^2 is above the exposure action value but below the exposure limit value.

Appendix D

Traffic light system

Some employers, working with machine manufacturers and suppliers, have developed a green/amber/red "traffic light" system, where each tool is clearly marked with a hand-arm vibration colour coding, dependent on the expected in-use vibration magnitude of each machine, one example of this coding scheme is illustrated in Table D.1.

Workers should be given training in the colour-coding scheme that is used, so that they can select vibration tools at a glance and know how long they can use the tool.

The success of the traffic light system is dependent on the quality of data used to determine the colour rating of each machine. The traffic light scheme may be based on measurements or manufacturer's declaration of vibration emission. If the vibration emission value is used, it should be multiplied by a factor of between 1 and 2, to account for uncertainty in the results from the standardised emission tests.

The use of a 'green' machine indicates that exposures are likely to be below the exposure action value. These exposures must not be assumed to be "safe". There may be a risk of hand-arm vibration injury for exposures below the exposure action value, and so other management controls must be used to ensure that workers are trained to understand and operate the system correctly, that the systems are actually correctly used, and that workers at risk do not develop symptoms of hand-arm vibration syndrome.

Table D.1 An example "traffic light" colour coding scheme to indicate acceptable daily durations of use for powered hand tools

Colour code	Time to reach EAV ($2.5 m/s^2$)	Time to reach ELV ($5 m/s^2$)
Red	Less than 30 mins	Less than 2 hours
Amber	30 minutes to 2 hours	2 to 8 hours
Green	More than 2 hours	More than 8 hours

Appendix E

Vibration exposure calculators

E.1 Daily exposure graph

The graph in Figure E.1 provides a simple method for looking up daily exposures or partial vibration exposures. Simply look on the graph for the *A*(8) line at or just above where the vibration magnitude value and exposure time lines meet.

The green area in Figure E.1 indicates exposures likely to below the exposure action value. These exposures must not be assumed to be "safe". There may be a risk of hand-arm vibration injury for exposures below the exposure action value, and so some exposures within the green area may cause vibration injury in some workers, especially after many years of exposure.

E.2 Exposure points system

An exposure "points" system is provided in PD CEN/TR 15350:2006 for simplifying hand-transmitted vibration exposure management. For any tool or process, the number of exposure points accumulated in an hour ($P_{E,1h}$ in points per hour) can be obtained from the vibration magnitude a_{hv} in m/s² using:

$$P_{E,1h} = 2a_{hv}^2$$

Exposure points are simply added together, so you can set a maximum number of exposure points for any person in one day.

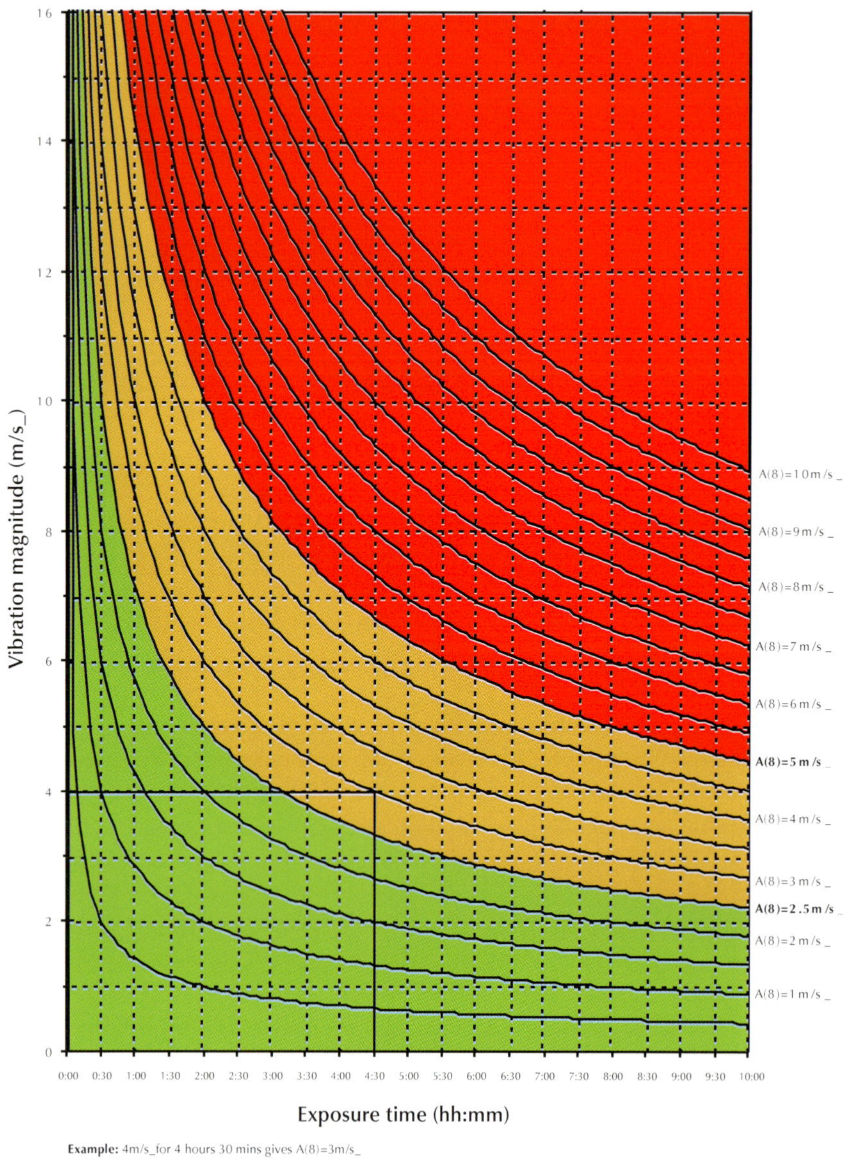

Figure E.1 Daily exposure graph for hand-transmitted vibration (after European Commission, 2008)

The exposure scores corresponding to the exposure action and limit values are:

- exposure action value (2.5 m/s^2) = 100 points;
- exposure limit value (5 m/s^2) = 400 points.

Alternatively, Figure E.2 provides a simple lookup table for exposure points.

E.3 Calculators available on the internet

The Health and Safety Executive provide a free calculator on the following website that simplifies the process of doing daily vibration exposure calculations:

- http://www.hse.gov.uk/vibration/hav/vibrationcalc.htm

The following alternative 'ready reckoner' for calculating daily vibration exposures is based on the points system explained in Section E.2:

- http://www.hse.gov.uk/vibration/hav/readyreckoner.htm

Acceleration (m/s_)	5m	15m	30m	1h	2h	3h	4h	5h	6h	8h	10h
20	67	200	400	800	1600	2400	3200	4000	4800	6400	8000
19.5	63	190	380	760	1500	2300	3050	3800	4550	6100	7600
19	60	180	360	720	1450	2150	2900	3600	4350	5800	7200
18.5	57	170	340	685	1350	2050	2750	3400	4100	5500	6850
18	54	160	325	650	1300	1950	2600	3250	3900	5200	6500
17.5	51	155	305	615	1250	1850	2450	3050	3700	4900	6150
17	48	145	290	580	1150	1750	2300	2900	3450	4600	5800
16.5	45	135	270	545	1100	1650	2200	2700	3250	4350	5450
16	43	130	255	510	1000	1550	2050	2550	3050	4100	5100
15.5	40	120	240	480	960	1450	1900	2400	2900	3850	4800
15	38	115	225	450	900	1350	1800	2250	2700	3600	4500
14.5	35	105	210	420	840	1250	1700	2100	2500	3350	4200
14	33	98	195	390	785	1200	1550	1950	2350	3150	3900
13.5	30	91	180	365	730	1100	1450	1800	2200	2900	3650
13	28	85	170	340	675	1000	1350	1700	2050	2700	3400
12.5	26	78	155	315	625	940	1250	1550	1900	2500	3150
12	24	72	145	290	575	865	1150	1450	1750	2300	2900
11.5	22	66	130	265	530	795	1050	1300	1600	2100	2650
11	20	61	120	240	485	725	970	1200	1450	1950	2400
10.5	18	55	110	220	440	660	880	1100	1300	1750	2200
10	17	50	100	200	400	600	800	1000	1200	1600	2000
9.5	15	45	90	180	360	540	720	905	1100	1450	1800
9	14	41	81	160	325	485	650	810	970	1300	1600
8.5	12	36	72	145	290	435	580	725	865	1150	1450
8	11	32	64	130	255	385	510	640	770	1000	1300
7.5	9	28	56	115	225	340	450	565	675	900	1150
7	8	25	49	98	195	295	390	490	590	785	980
6.5	7	21	42	85	170	255	340	425	505	675	845
6	6	18	36	72	145	215	290	360	430	575	720
5.5	5	15	30	61	120	180	240	305	365	485	605
5	4	13	25	50	100	150	200	250	300	400	500
4.5	3	10	20	41	81	120	160	205	245	325	405
4	3	8	16	32	64	96	130	160	190	255	320
3.5	2	6	12	25	49	74	98	125	145	195	245
3	2	5	9	18	36	54	72	90	110	145	180
2.5	1	3	6	13	25	38	50	63	75	100	125

Daily exposure time

Figure E.2 Exposure points lookup table for hand-transmitted vibration (the values are rounded to the nearest whole number), from European Commission (2008).

Appendix F

Format for reporting results of a survey of shipboard hand-transmitted vibration

Whilst the 2007 Vibration Regulations do not specify the format for any hand-transmitted vibration survey report, it is suggested that a report in the form set out below might usefully be carried onboard the vessel to which it applies.

A hand-transmitted vibration assessment should be planned and carried out by a competent person, who then prepares a suitable and sufficient report of the findings. The vibration assessment should identify workers by name or by task, and report the frequency-weighted vibration magnitudes to which they are exposed and for how long. The assessment should show the location of the workers when they are at risk, as well as the tools or controls that produce the hand-transmitted vibration.

Table F.1 provides information about the survey, including characteristics of the vessel, the person carrying out the assessment and the equipment used to measure hand-transmitted vibration. Enter the acceleration magnitudes indicated from each accelerometer during calibration checks carried out before the measurements: this demonstrates that a calibration check was actually performed.

Sketches or drawings should be provided to show numbered positions of the vibration measurement locations, which are referred to in the tables below. A list of tools on which measurements were made should also be provided, showing how the accelerometers were attached to the tool.

Table F.2 is a worksheet for recording hand-transmitted vibration measurements for crew members during each daily activity that involves exposure to hand-transmitted vibration. Partial vibration exposures should be entered for each activity, as well as the overall $A(8)$ daily vibration exposures calculated from the partial $A(8)$ values.

Table F.3 is intended to summarise the measurements on individual tools. The maximum recorded frequency-weighted vibration magnitudes should be entered for each measurement axis, as well as the overall a_{hv}.

Based on observations made during the measurements, the hand-transmitted vibration assessor may be able to recommend measures for controlling the vibration exposures. Recommendations for vibration reduction measures should be listed in Table F.4.

Table F.5 provides a summary of the daily exposures to hand-transmitted vibration from the individual worksheets (Table F.2), and indicates whether these exceed either the exposure action value (EAV) or exposure limit value (ELV) in the 2007 Vibration Regulations.

If frequency analysis is available, it is recommended that example frequency spectra of the unweighted accelerations in each axis should be included with the report.

Table F.1 Summary information about the hand-transmitted vibration survey

OCCUPATIONAL HEALTH AND SAFETY INSPECTION
HAND-TRANSMITTED VIBRATION ASSESSMENT
UNITED KINGDOM REGISTERED VESSELS

Name of vessel		Type of vessel	
Company or owner		Port of registry	
Official number		IMO number	

Accelerometers (make and model)		Serial numbers	
Vibration meter/ amplifiers/recorder (make and model)		Serial numbers	
Acquisition and analysis software		Serial numbers	

Calibrator (make and model)		Serial number	
Calibration frequency (Hz)		Calibration magnitude (ms^{-2})	
Recorded calibration magnitude (ms^{-2})	*x*-axis:	*y*-axis:	*z*-axis:

Date of vibration measurements		Start Time and Finish Time	
Calibration dates and traceability			

Vibration assessor		Official Stamp
Assessor's signature		
Assessor's office address		
Date of report		

General Notes/Comments *create more space as needed*

Table F.2 Worksheet for recording hand-transmitted vibration measurements and assessments for crew members

vessel:	
date:	surveyor:
vessel location during measurements:	

name of crew member or job	measurement location (state if on seat or deck) and measurement conditions	position on ship plan	time of measure-ment	sample duration (s, m or h)	frequency-weighted acceleration in each axis (ms-2 r.m.s.)			aw (ms^{-2} r.m.s.)	exposure duration (s, m or h)	$A(8)$ (ms^{-2} r.m.s.)	see remarks below
					a_{wx}	a_{wy}	a_{wz}				
Daily vibration exposure $A(8)$:											

remark number (from above)	remarks

Table F.3 Summary of hand-transmitted vibration magnitudes

location (state if on seat or deck) and measurement conditions	position on ship plan	frequency-weighted acceleration in each axis (ms^{-2} r.m.s.)			a_w (ms^{-2} r.m.s.)
		a_{wx}	a_{wy}	a_{wz}	
create more rows as needed					

Table F.4 Vibration reduction measures

Location	position on ship plan	technical measures	organisational measures
create more rows as needed			

Table F.5 Daily exposures to hand-transmitted vibration

name of crew member or job	activity making greatest contribution to whole-body vibration exposure	position on ship plan	daily vibration exposure, A(8) (ms^{-2} r.m.s.)	is EAV exceeded? (yes/no)	is ELV exceeded? (yes/no)
create more rows as needed					

Appendix G

Health risks, signs and symptoms

This appendix is reproduced from the Non-binding guide to good practice with a view to implementation of Directive 2002/44/EC on the minimum health and safety requirements regarding the exposure of workers to the risks arising from physical agents (vibrations) (European Commission, 2008).

G.1 The hand-arm vibration syndrome

Workers exposed regularly to excessive hand-arm-transmitted vibration may suffer in the long term with disturbances to finger blood flow and to the neurological and locomotor functions of the hand and arm. The term hand-arm vibration syndrome is used to refer to these complex disorders.

Hand-arm vibration syndrome has an impact on social and family life. Periodic attacks of impaired blood circulation will take place not only at work, but also during activities such as car washing or watching outdoor sports. Everyday tasks, for example managing small buttons on clothes may become difficult.

Vascular disorders, neurological disorders and bone and joints abnormalities caused by hand-transmitted-arm vibration are recognized occupational diseases in the UK and in several European countries.

G.2 Vascular disorders

Workers exposed to hand-transmitted-arm vibration may complain of episodes of whitening (blanching) of the fingers, usually triggered by cold exposure. This symptom is caused by temporary closing down of blood circulation to the fingers.

Various terms have been used to describe vibration-induced vascular disorders:

- dead or white finger,
- Raynaud's phenomenon of occupational origin,
- vibration-induced white finger.

Initially attacks of blanching involve the tips of one or more fingers, but, with continued exposure to vibration, the blanching can extend to the base of the fingers. As the blood flow returns to the fingers (this is commonly initiated by warmth or local massage) the fingers turn red, and are often painful. The blanching attacks are more common in winter than in summer. The duration varies with the intensity of the vibration stimuli from a few minutes to more than one hour.

If vibration exposure continues, the blanching attacks become more frequent affecting more of the fingers. The attacks may occur all year around with quite small reductions of temperature. During a blanching attack the affected worker can experience a complete loss of touch sensation and manipulative dexterity, which can interfere with work activity increasing the risk for acute injuries due to accidents.

Epidemiological studies have demonstrated that the probability and severity of blanching is influenced by the characteristics of vibration exposure and duration of exposure, the type of tool and work process, the environmental conditions (temperature, air flow, humidity, noise), some biodynamic and ergonomic factors (grip force, push force, arm position), and various individual characteristics (individual susceptibility, diseases and agents such as smoking and certain medicines that affect peripheral circulation).

G.3 Neurological disorders

Workers exposed to hand-transmitted arm vibration may experience tingling and numbness in their fingers and hands. If vibration exposure continues, these symptoms tend to worsen and can interfere with work capacity and life activities. Vibration-exposed workers may exhibit a reduction in the normal sense of touch and temperature as well as an impairment of manual dexterity.

G.4 Carpal-tunnel syndrome

Epidemiological research in workers has also shown that use of vibrating tools in combination with repetitive movements, forceful gripping, awkward postures may increase the risk of carpal tunnel syndrome.

G.5 Musculoskeletal disorders

Workers with prolonged exposure to vibration may complain of muscular weakness, pain in the hands and arms, and diminished muscle strength. These disorders seem to be related to ergonomic stress factors arising from heavy manual work.

Excess occurrence of wrist and elbow osteoarthritis as well as hardening of soft tissue (ossification) at the sites of tendon attachment, mostly at the elbow, have been found in miners, road construction workers and metal-working operators of percussive tools.

Other work-related disorders have been reported in vibration-exposed workers, such as inflammation of tendons (tendonitis) and their sheaths in the upper limbs, and Dupuytren's contracture, a disease of the fascial tissues of the palm of the hand.

Appendix H

Health surveillance for hand-transmitted vibration

The following appendix is reproduced from Health and Safety Executive (2008).

H.1 Providing health surveillance

You must provide health surveillance for all your employees who, despite your action to control the risk, are likely to be regularly exposed above the exposure action value or are considered to be at risk for any other reason. The purpose of health surveillance is to:

- identify anyone exposed or about to be exposed to hand-arm vibration who may be at particular risk, for example people with blood circulatory diseases such as Raynaud's disease;
- identify any vibration-related disease at an early stage in employees regularly exposed to hand-arm vibration;
- help you prevent disease progression and eventual disability;
- help people stay in work;
- check the effectiveness of your vibration control measures.

You should consult with your trade union safety representative, or employee representative, and the employees concerned before introducing health surveillance. It is important that your employees understand that the aim of health surveillance is to protect them from developing advanced symptoms of ill health so that they can continue to work. You will need their understanding and co-operation if health surveillance is to be effective.

H.2 How can I arrange health surveillance?

Basic health surveillance consists of regularly seeking information about early symptoms of ill health by using a questionnaire. It may help you keep costs down if you carry out this function yourself, referring any positive responses to an occupational health service provider.

Alternatively, you could ask an occupational health service provider to provide a complete service on your behalf. You should be able to find details of occupational health service providers from your trade association, your local telephone directory, the internet or your nearest HSE office.

H.3 What should I expect from an occupational health service provider?

A suitable occupational health service provider will have training and experience in health surveillance for hand-arm vibration.

They should be able to:

- advise you on a suitable health surveillance programme for your employees;
- set up the programme;
- provide the necessary training and supervision for your staff if they are going to help with the basic health surveillance;
- provide suitably qualified and experienced staff to carry out the higher level health surveillance;
- provide you with reports on your employees' fitness to continue work with vibration exposure.

H.4 What do I have to do with the results of health surveillance?

You will need to:

- keep records of the health surveillance and fitness for work advice provided for each employee (but not the confidential medical records which are kept by the doctor). An MCA surveyor is entitled to ask to see the health surveillance records as part of their checks that you are complying with these Regulations;
- make employees' records available to them;
- act upon any recommendations made by the doctor about employees' continued exposure to vibration;
- use the results to review and, if necessary, revise your risk assessment, including your plans to control risks;

- discuss any changes to your risk assessment with your trade union safety representative or employee representative;
- notify the relevant enforcing authority when advised in writing by a doctor that an employee in a listed occupation has HAVS or carpal tunnel syndrome, as required by the Reporting of Injuries, Diseases and Dangerous Occurrences Regulations 1995 (RIDDOR). [Note: These regulations only apply to ships operating solely within UK inland waters, and not to sea-going ships. Cases of HAVS arising from certain occupations and work activities (which are listed in SI 1995/3163, schedule 3), and of carpal tunnel syndrome associated with exposure to vibration, should be reported to the RIDDOR incident contact centre (http://www.riddor.gov.uk). The listed occupations for reporting of HAVS include those involving use of rotary tools in grinding and the use of percussive tools in riveting, caulking, and chipping].

H.5 Further Information on Health surveillance

For further downloadable information and questionnaires that can be used by employers or by health professionals see:

http://www.hse.gov.uk/vibration/hav/advicetoemployers/healthsurveillance.htmNotes

Notes

Notes